NATIONALISM
AND THE IMAGINATION

Gayatri Chakravorty Spivak

NATIONALISM AND THE IMAGINATION

LONDON NEW YORK CALCUTTA

Seagull Books, 2015

First published in paperback edition in 2015

© Gayatri Chakravorty Spivak, 2010

ISBN   978 0 8574 2 318 4

British Library Cataloguing-in-Publication Data
A catalogue record for this book is available
from the British Library

Typeset by Seagull Books, Calcutta, India
Printed and bound by Hyam Enterprises, Calcutta, India

NATIONALISM AND THE IMAGINATION

I am tremendously honoured to be a guest of the Centre for Advanced Study here in Sofia—Alexander Kiossev knows that I really tried to make this happen. What I am going to read refers to India, and I would say that the Indian example is not unique but different. Your history would probably not produce the kind of nationalism that the history of India did immediately after Independence.

Alexander gave me a paper this afternoon titled 'Ensuring Compatibility Respecting Differences'. That's what I will be asking you to do as you hear me. You say that I have been invited partly because the group is interested in translation. You will have to translate the circumstances as I speak.

I remember Independence—I was very young, but I was precocious—and it was an incredible event. But my earliest memories are of famine: skeletal bodies dying in the streets, crawling to the back door begging for starch. This was the great artificial famine created by the British to feed the military in the Pacific Theater during the Second World War. A bit later, I learned the extraordinary songs of the Indian People's Theatre Association—the famous IPTA. Why were they political? One of you was asking me if literary representations could be political. In this case what happened was that section 144 of the Penal Code, enforcing preventive detention, was put in place to control resistance. But the British authorities did not understand the Indian languages, so theatre fell through the cracks and the IPTA survived as a political organization. Like most Bengali children, I learned their extraordinary songs, and I will quote the refrain that haunts our cultural memory: 'We won't give any more rice, for this rice, sown in blood, is our life.' I didn't connect it to the British—only to the class struggle.

The British were mentioned only in that street rhyme about the Japanese: 'Do re mi fa so la ti / dropped the bomb on the Japanese. / In the bomb, a cobra snake / the British scream:

"Oh Lord, help, help!" ' The Japanese, we thought in Bengal, were bringing the British to their knees, and we admired them for it. Kolkata was evacuated at the time of my birth for fear of Japanese bombings. You folks were first with the Axis powers and then with the Allies. For us, it was happening at the same time. The largest number of dead in the Second World War was Indian soldiers fighting for the British. On the other hand, at India's eastern edge, there was the alliance with the Japanese and the Axis powers. Subhas Chandra Bose, a family friend, was a friend of the Japanese and the leader of the Indian National Army. He went off to Japan and from there to Germany and married a German woman. (Kolkata airport is named after him.) So there was this synchronic commitment to the Allies and to the Axis. The lines were crossed. For the Europeans it was the Holocaust, but for us it was a world war, the end of colonialism perhaps.

As I said, Kolkata was evacuated at the time of my birth. My mother, however, refused to leave. She said, 'I will have my child in Kolkata.' My grandmother stayed too, so I was born in the city. In 1946, I entered kindergarten. In October, school closed. We lived right on the border of a Muslim quarter, on the edge of Syed Amir Ali Avenue. Those areas were among the cruellest sites of the Hindu–Muslim violence. It was a politically mobilized violence—the country was going to be divided and so, people with whom we had lived forever, for centuries, in conflictual coexistence, suddenly became enemies. I was four years old, and these are my first memories. The cries would go up, celebrating the divine in a Hindu or a Muslim way. Even we children knew that each cry meant a knife thrust, a machete blow. (Those riots were not fought with guns.) It was the working-class people, the underclass people who were mobilized, because the British and the upper-class folks had made a pact to separate the land. There was blood on the streets and I don't mean that metaphorically. These are my earliest memories: famine and blood on the streets.

My parents were ecumenical secularist anticasteists. I am an atheist but was born in a Hindu family. At night, the house was full of Muslim women and children who my father had brought in from the neighbouring low-income housing estate (which in those days was called a slum but that's politically incorrect now). The men and my father would be on the terrace.

By contrast, Independence was a polite affair. Elation in the conversation of the elders, interminable political discussions. Remember, we were 300 years under the Islamic empire and then 200 years under the British. So it was big. Marching along wearing white and blue, waving flags, singing the inevitable songs by Tagore. The important event was Partition, the division of the country. Mother was out at dawn, at the minor railway station as the trains came in from the East, busy with refugee relief and rehabilitation, coming home battered in the middle of the evening. Overnight, Kolkata became a burdened city; even its speech patterns changed. If these were the recollections of Independence, the nationalist message in the streets created schizophrenia.

If there is anyone my age in the audience who grew up in Kolkata (I know there isn't, but I say it anyway) and did not lead a hopelessly sheltered life, she will remember that, in addition to the Hindi film songs, the plays that were broadcast over the loudspeaker at every Durga Puja—Durga Puja is our commercialized high holiday, a major event of ideological production—were *Siraj-ud-daula*, the story of the unhappy betrayed Nawab, the Muslim king who fought with Robert Clive, the man who brought in territorial imperialism into India; and *Mebar Patan*, a play written in my family a hundred years ago coding the Rajputs ambiguously, so that the Muslims became an ambiguous analogue to the British. I thought you would appreciate this because of your Ottoman connections. The British are our enemy, so are the Muslims—ambiguous, for the British may suddenly become our saviour!

This hardy residual of the Muslim as not only enemy but evil is still being worked by the Hindu right. To translate the sentiment of a famous song from *Mebar Patan*: voluptuous sex is bad; mothers and wives are good and must be protected; the Muslim are the enemy. Yet this play was by a famous liberationist poet, whose songs are sung every Independence Day. I will translate a few sentences: 'Does it become you to lie down in despicable lust, when town and country are in fear of the enemy? Upon that chest devastated by the blows of the Muslim, are the arms of the paramour an appropriate adornment? Who will care to preserve his life, when mother and wife are in danger? To arms! To arms!'

What my adolescent mind, growing into adulthood in the Kolkata of the 50s, began to grasp, was that nationalism was tied to the circumstances of one's birth, its recoding in terms of migration, marriage and history disappearing into claims to ancient birth. Its ingredients are to be found in the assumptions of what I later learned to call reproductive heteronormativity. That is why I quoted the song: reproductive heteronormativity is in its every pore. And the important question was: are you natural or naturalized? George Bush or Madeline Albright? Bulgarian or Turk? When I look at Todor Zhivkov's arguments that Bulgarians had an organized state before the Russians, they were Christians before the Russians, I think of this: ancient claims to things becoming nationalism by virtue of a shared ancestry.

As I was growing up, then, I realized that nationalism was related to reproductive heteronormativity as a source of legitimacy. As I moved to the United States and became active around the world, I realized that the alibi for transnational agencies was nationalism in the developing world. Gender was an alibi here, even for military intervention in the name of humanitarian intervention. I believe with Eric Hobsbawm that there is no nation before nationalism. But I do not locate nationalism as he does in the late eighteenth century.

When and how does the love of mother tongue, the love of my little corner of ground become the nation thing? I say nation thing rather than nationalism because something like nations, collectivities bound by birth, that allowed in strangers gingerly, has been in existence long before nationalism came around. State formations change but the nation thing moves through historical displacements, and I think Hannah Arendt was altogether perceptive in suggesting that the putting together of nationalism with the abstract structure of the state was an experiment or a happening that has a limited history and a limited future. We are living, as Jürgen Habermas says, in post-national situations. We'll see.

To return to my question: when and how does the love of mother tongue change like this? Let us revise. Pared down, when and how does the love of mother tongue, the love of my little corner of ground, become the nation thing? Pared down, this love or attachment is more like comfort. It is not really the declared love of country, full-blown nationalism. Let us revise: when and how does the comfort felt in one's mother tongue and the comfort felt in one's corner of the sidewalk, a patch of ground—and as a New Yorker I will add a fire hydrant or a church door—transform itself into the nation thing?

Let us try to pare it down a little further. This rock-bottom comfort, with which the nation thing conjures, is not a positive affect. I learned this in the 18 years of my friendship with the Indian aboriginals for and with who I worked. I worked for them as a teacher and a trainer of teachers, and it is not my habit to romanticize my students or their parents. To return to my argument: this rock-bottom comfort in one's language and one's home, with which nationalism conjures, is not a positive affect. (I would not have known this as a metropolitan Kolkata person at the time of Independence, at the inception of the new nation-state from an established nationalism.) When there is nothing but this, its working is simply a thereness. Please remember, I am not talking about resistance groups but of people who accept wretchedness as normality. That's the subaltern, those are the folks that I worked with. I learned this from below. When this comfort is taken away, there is a feeling of helplessness, loss of orientation, dependency, but no nation thing. At the extreme, perhaps a banding together, making common cause through reinvention of something like religious discourse into an ethics that can condone violence. This is the work of the early subaltern studies group of historians: tracking religion being brought to crisis as militancy that can condone a certain kind of violence—but not nationalism.

We are so used to the cliché that there is nothing private outside of Europe that we are unable to recognize that in this sphere, if it can be called that, it is the guarantee of the profound, bottom-line shared unease of the removal of comfort that solders the band together. We have to understand that in a country as large and as socially layered as mine, nationalism doesn't work right through.

The nationalism I have been describing operates in the public sphere. But the subaltern affect where it finds its mobilizing is private, though this possibility of the private is not derived from a sense of the public. An underived private, which is very difficult for Europe to think. Women, men and queers are not necessarily divided along the public–private line everywhere. I have already let slip that nationalism is a recoding of this underived private as the antonym of the public sphere. When you begin to think nationalism, this underived private has been recoded and reterritorialized as the antonym of the public. As if it is the opposite of the public. This shift is historical, of course, but it is also logical. The subaltern folks I am talking about are in our present but are kept pre-modern.

I will not rehearse here the mostly Hegelian historical story of the emergence of the public sphere. In whatever nationalist colours they are dressed, whether chronological or logical, the impulse to nationalism is 'we must control the workings of our own public sphere.' The reclaiming of the past is in that interest. Sometimes, nationalism leads to the resolve to control others' public spheres, although this is not a necessary outcome. With this comes the necessary though often unacknowledged sense of being unique and, alas, better—it's a quick shift— because one was born this way.

I have here offered a reading of nationalism that allows us to see why, although it is the condition and effect of the public sphere, nationalisms are not able to work with the founding logic of the public sphere: that all reason is one. They are secured by the private conviction of special birth and hop right from the underived private comfort which is just a thereness in one's corner.

If nationalism secures itself by an appeal to the most private, democracy in its most convenient and ascertainable form is secured by the most trivially public universal—each equals one. That flimsy arithmetic, unprotected by rational choice, can also be manipulated by nationalism. I am not convinced that the story of human movement to a greater control of the public sphere is necessarily a story of progress. The religion–science debate makes this assumption, forgetting that the imagination, literature and the arts belong neither to reason nor to unreason. That literature and the arts can support an advanced nationalism is no secret. They join in the task of a massive rememoration project, saying 'we all suffered this way, you remember, this is what happened, you remember,' so that history is turned into cultural memory. Literature takes it further by suggesting that we have all passed through the same glorious past, the same grand national liberation battles, the same religious tolerance and so on. I am going to suggest by the end of this, because sometimes I am misunderstood, that the literary imagination can impact on de-transcendentalizing nationalism. That is not what I am discussing here. I am supporting the cliché that imagination feeds nationalism, and going forward towards the literary imagination and teaching the humanities, through the teaching of the humanities, to prepare the readerly imagination to receive the literary and thus go beyond the self-identity of nationalism towards the complex textuality of the international. I will come to that later.

I want now to share with you a lesson learned from the oral-formulaic. If the main thing about narrative is sequence, the main thing about the oral-formulaic is equivalence. Equivalence here does not mean value in the sense of commensurate—that was the Marxist definition in the economic sphere. I am speaking of value in a more colloquial sense. We learn from narrative by working at the sequence. We learn in the oral by mastering equivalence. Some years ago, Roman Jakobsen offered equivalence as the poetic function. In typical modernist fashion, he thought equivalence lifted the burden of meaning. My experience with the oral-formulaic presentation of Sabar women, the groups that I used to train teachers for until the local landlord took the schools away from me and handed them to the corporate sector to bring up casual labour, has convinced me that it is the inventiveness in equivalence that makes something happen beyond the tonal and verbal monotony that turn off many literate sympathizers. The Sabar women are members of a tiny and unrepresentative group among India's 82 million aboriginals. They still practise the oral-formulaic, although they will soon forget this centuries-old skill. The hold upon orality is gender-divided here. The men's access to the outside world is wretched, working day labour for the Hindu villages; and, since they don't themselves know that there are 24 hours in the day, they are cheated constantly. That is why I used to have these schools, to give the subaltern a chance at hegemony.

The men's access to the outside world is nonetheless more 'open'. When the men sing, the archived yet inventive memory of the oral-formulaic approaches rote. The men, and this is a very important distinction, inhabit enforced illiteracy rather than an orality at home with itself and with the great genealogical memories. The women, because of the peculiar situation of gender, were still practising the oral-formulaic.

The pre-colonial name for the area where I worked is Manbhum. It is not the name now. In the adjoining state of Jharkhand there is Singbhum, not the name on the map now. Pre-colonial names. To the south is Birbhum, etc. Imagine the frisson of delight that passed through me the first time I heard these women weave a verse that began: *Manbhumer Man raja*—'King Man of Manbhum'—using the pre-colonial name of this place that nobody uses. The next line was even more delightful: *Kolkatar rajar pathorer dalan bé*—'the King of Kolkata has a stone mansion.' Kolkata was in the place of what I am calling 'inventive equivalence'.

They were going to Kolkata, a little group for a fair, so they were honouring the King of Kolkata by preparing these songs. Kolkata is my home-town and I was thinking, as I sang with the women in that remote room—with no furniture, no doors and windows, no plumbing, no elec-tricity, only a six-foot by nine-foot sheet of poly-thene in some way associated with chemical fertilizer—who would the King of Kolkata be? Kolkata is a colonial city and, unlike older Indian cities, had never had a Nawab; indeed, unlike Bardhaman, Krishnanagar, Srihatta (Sylhet), Jashor or Mymensingh, it had never had a Hindu Raja either. But the women were singing 'The King of Kolkata has a stone man-sion,' where Kolkata occupied the place of a shifter, and who was I to contradict it?

Mahasweta Devi used to organize tribal fairs in Kolkata where people came to buy handicrafts. That's where they were going, and that's why they were preparing. The building where these fairs took place in Kolkata is called *tathhokendra*—Information Centre. 'What is the name of that place?' one of the women asked me. 'Tathhokendra,' I said. They produced the line: *Tathhokendrer rajar patharer dalan bé*—the King of the Information Centre has a stone mansion. It would be better to keep it 'Kolkata' I said, inwardly noting with wonderment that although they knew that Kolkata was a city with zoos and parks and streets and the Information Centre only a building, and although they knew that no king had power over them, the concept of sovereignty, that would put a space in apposition to archaic Manbhum or Barabhum, applied to both equally.

Here, then, is a thinking without nation, space-names as shifters, in a mythic geography, because of the power of the formulaic. In internationality the nation-state supposedly has such equivalence, now rationally determined. In globalization, no, because there the medium of value is capital. This geography was not, realistically speaking, mythic. This is the sort of intuition that Jean-François Lyotard, and before him Marshall McLuhan, had claimed for postmodernity, jumping the printed book in between. Their politics ignored the texture of subalternity, equating it with internationality with no gap. Lyotard tried, in *The Differend* (1983) to undo it, but most readers did not make the connection. Without the benefit of postmodern argumentation, such geographical intuitions are defined as pre-modern and by Hobsbawm as pre-political. The group I worked with is not tied to counter-globalization. They are too subaltern to attack the indigenous knowledge or population control people, and their avoidance of chemical fertilizers or pesticides (now destroyed) was then too recent and not connected to large-scale agriculture.

If, however, they had been connected to counter-globalization then they would accede to a nationalist moment—because the activist workers would speak nation to them. My account is of a nationalist moment in affective collectivity with no historical base, ultimately productive of neither nationalism nor counter-globalization but, rather, of obedience disguised as self-help.

One year, I had added a line to their singing of locators—names of 'their' village (the Hindus deny them entry there), their district and so on—'West Bengal is my state, India is my nation.' This is how:

A group of women, larger than the group that went to Kolkata, and I walked to the central village of the area. One of the protocols of these two-and-a-half-hour walks was that we sing at the tops of our voices. I longed for a camera person—I am joking, I have never wanted anybody there—as these aboriginal women and I walked in the sparsely forested plains of Manbhum, screaming 'India is my country'—*bharat henak desh bé*—again and again and again—the moment of access to nationalism—Gayatri Spivak travelling with the subaltern would then be caught on camera. Except that it wasn't access to nationalism, of course. The oral-formulaic can appropriate material of all sorts into its machine, robbing the content of its epistemic charge. If it does not fit the inventiveness of the occasion, and this is what Jakobsen thought was the poetic, that takes away meaning and is only equivalence. Indeed West Bengal or Paschim Banga—the name of the state—has long been changed by these women into Paschim Mangal, a meaningless phrase with a Sanskrit-like aura. And the lines are only sung when Shukhoda wants to show me that she loves me still. (With the schools closed, I may never see them again.) I am not asking us to imitate the oral-formulaic—I am suggesting that the principle of inventive equivalence should be at the core of the comparativist impulse. It is not all that a fully elaborated comparativism does. But the principle would be on the way to the effacement of the hierarchical functioning of current Comparative Literature which measures in terms of a standard at whose heart is Western European nationalisms. Standing in the airport of Paris, I have been turned off by the accent of upstate New

York and turned to my mother and said in Bengali, 'You can't listen to this.' But she chided me, also in Bengali, 'Dear, it is a mother tongue.' That sense, that the language learned first through the infantile mechanism is every language, not just one's own, is equivalence. You cannot be an enemy of English. People say easily 'English is globalization. It is destroying cultural specificity.' Here is equivalence. It is not equalization, it is not a removal of difference, it is not cutting the unfamiliar down to the familiar. It is perhaps learning to acknowledge that other things can occupy the unique place of the example of my first language. This is hard. It's not an easy intuition to develop, yet this need not take away the comfort in one's food, one's language, one's corner of the world. Although even this the nomad can give up. Remember Edward Said quoting Hugo of St Victor: 'The man who finds his homeland sweet is still a tender beginner; he to whom every soil is as his native one is already strong; but he is perfect to whom the entire world is as a foreign land.' The human being can give up even the facticity of language, but comparativism need not. What a comparativism based on equivalence attempts to undermine is the possessiveness, the exclusiveness, the isolationist expansionism of mere nationalism.

Why is the first learned language so important? Because it teaches every human infant to negotiate the public and the private outside of the public–private divide as we have inherited it from the legacy of European history. Language has a history; it is public before our births and will continue so after our deaths. Yet every infant invents it and makes it the most private thing, touching the very interiority of the heart. On a more superficial level, it is this underived private that nationalism appropriates. A multi-lingual republic like mine with a national language for communication—Hindi—can, in the literary sphere work, the admirable comparativist move—my mother's move—recognizing that there are many first languages—24 if you don't count the aboriginals, 850 if you do. If we think that postcolonial literature is simply another name of post-imperial literature in the British Commonwealth, the former British Empire, I am afraid that move is not made.

The British Commonwealth has an association called the Commonwealth Association. It is supposedly for the study of languages as well, and the Commonwealth has many. Cyprus, Malta, Burkina Faso, all these places were in the Commonwealth. So were 15 African nations. But the Association mainly becomes a clearing-house for the exuberance of Global English. It should, of course, welcome a consideration of textual analyses of cultural work in the various languages of Africa and India. The tendency should now go beyond the question of translation into the possibility for the members of the old British Commonwealth to re-open what was closed by colonialism: linguistic diversity. The media of communication can remain English— that gift of colonialism we can accept as convenience. But the work must become comparativist. That would indeed be the Empire writing back in tongues.

Here is Maryse Condé, a francophone novelist from Guadeloupe. In the passage below, she is picturing the Caribbean upper class confronting subaltern Africa. An undisclosed West African subaltern speaker, possibly feminine, says to the French-speaking upper-class Véronique from Martinique: 'What strangeness that country [*quelle étrangeté ce pays*] which produced [*qui ne produisait*] neither Mandingo, nor Fulani, nor Toucouleur, nor Serer, nor Woloff, nor Toma, nor Guerze, nor Fang, nor Fon, nor Bété, nor Ewe, nor Dagbani, nor Yoruba, nor Mina, nor Ibo. And it was still Blacks who lived there [*Et c'étaient tout de même des Noirs qui vivaient là*!].' The young woman passes this by, noting only her pleasure at being complimented on her appearance: ' "Are all the women of that country as pretty as Mademoiselle?" I got a silly pleasure out of hearing this.'

Of course, Bulgaria has been incredibly conscious of its languages, an amazing phenomenon. So, to an extent, this doesn't apply but, on the other hand, remember equivalence. You must translate. You must think—there is Africa. As you were saying, there would not be interest among students if African languages were introduced here. Is it possible to change this?

Veronica does not hear the subaltern African woman's question. If the association does not pick up the challenge of Comparative Literature, then literatures in the Indian languages, like many literatures in regional languages, will not flourish; they cannot do so on their own. That is why, this afternoon, I said to my friend who is working on Indian literature in English, 'Don't kill us.' If you compare the advances paid to a writer like Vikram Seth with the kind of money that the Indian language literatures make, it's amazing that these latter are still so powerful. A terrible sociology of knowledge is taking the name 'Indian' away from them. A Columbia student recently offered a field called Indian Literature for his doctoral examination. 'Surely you mean Indian literature in English?' asked I. And he said, 'I am following Amit Chaudhuri's definition that only literature in English written on the subcontinent can qualify as Indian.' Rushdie's word for the literature of all the Indian languages that he could not read was 'parochial'. Can one not suggest that the repeated narration of the immigrant experience, however varied the style, taking the relay from the presentation of India the exotic, into India-Britain or India-America as fusion, always focused on the writer's own corner, is also a bit 'parochial'?

This is sociology of knowledge at work, creolizing the Indian languages artificially to English, undoing the separated yet hierarchically shared histories of North and South Indian literatures. In a double bind with the uniformization of English, I have long proposed not just an Indian Comparative Literature in a nationalist ghetto, but comparative literature as such, productively undoing the mono-cultures of the British Empire, all empires and all revolutions. Women from Central Asia come to the United States, come to Columbia, because we have a big Harriman Institute—it used to be Soviet Studies but is now Post-Soviet Studies. They often come to talk to me, because I do feminism and Tashkent is close to India. One of the things they say is that they can't talk to their grandmothers, because they all speak Russian and their native language is no longer nuanced for them. If one begins to establish the outlines of a global comparative literature, one can at least hope that the deep linguistic consequences of the largely female sovietization described in Gregory Massell's *Surrogate Proletariat* (1974) can come undone. In this context, I recall Marx's very well-known words: 'The beginner

who has learned a new language always re-
translates it into his mother tongue. He can
only be said to have appropriated the spirit of
the new language and to be able to produce in
it freely when he can manipulate it without
reference to the old and when he forgets the
language planted in him while using the new
one.' I am not translating from the Bengali when
I am speaking English. I cannot translate my
own Bengali into English—what I publish in
Bengali, remains in Bengali; other people find it
very difficult to translate too. 'To be able to produce in it freely when he can manipulate it without reference to the old and when he forgets the
language planted in him while using the new
one.' This is what a translator should be—someone who can forget translation. This is a literal
description both of good comparative literature
and the kind of energy the dominant unifying

languages can command. We cannot learn all the languages of the world in this kind of depth. But we can learn two: $n+1$. And, in the process, restore the relief map of the world, flattened under one imperial formation. And it doesn't matter what you call that empire.

Nationalism is the product of a collective imagination constructed through rememoration. It is the comparativist imagination that undoes that possessive spell. The imagination must be trained to take pleasure in such strenuous play. Yet social priorities today are not such that higher education in the humanities can prosper, certainly not in India as it is rising to take its place as a competitor in a 'developed' world, and certainly not in the United States. The humanities are progressively trivialized and/or self-trivialized into belles-lettristic or quantitative work. If I have learned anything in my 45 years of full-time teaching, it is the tragedy of the trivialization of the humanities, a kind of cultural death. So unless the polity values the teaching of literature in this way rather than just literary history and content and a fake scientism, the imagination will not be nourished.

I am going to talk now about a few metaphors and then come to an end.

The first is time and woman. A general temporizing narrative enables individual and collective life. Simon Gikandi has worked with narratives that support genocide in the African context (he is himself a Kenyan) and how the African can intervene in these narratives. Israel supports legitimized state violence by the so-called biblical narrative, but this is much broader.

The role of women, through their placing in the reproductive heteronormativity that supports nationalisms, is of great significance in this general temporizing narrative. When we are born, we are born into the possibility of timing, temporalization—we are in time. This possibility we can grasp only by temporizing, thinking and feeling a before, which, through a now, will fall due in an after. Our first languaging seems almost coeval with this, for we are also born into it. Since, as I said, it has a before before us, we take from its already-thereness. And since we can give meaning in it, we can think ourselves into the falling-due of the future by way of it. It is this thought, of giving and taking, that is the idiomatic story of time into which the imposition of identities must be accommodated. Since it is usually our mothers who seem to bring us into temporalization, by giving birth, our temporizing often marks that particular intuition of origin by coding and re-coding the mother, by computing possible futures through investing or manipulating womanspace. The daughtership of the nation is bound up with that very recoding. Another example of temporizing towards a future that will fall due is of women as holding the future of the nation in their wombs. It comes from the obvious narrative of marriage. Language, mother, daughter, nation, marriage. Themes with which I began, where we begin. The task of the literary imagination in the contemporary is the persistent de-transcendentalization of such figures. In other words, if you study this graphic as text, you can keep it framed in the imaginary, rather than see it as the ineffable cultural 'reality' that drives the public sphere, the civic structure that holds the state. 'Culture' is a rusing signifier. If you are committed to 'cultural' nationalism, while your 'civic' nationalism is committed to a Group of Eight [G8] state, it is possible, though not necessary, that you work against redistributive social justice in the 'culturally' chosen nation. This is very important as one moves up into neo-liberal globalization.

Let me repeat: If we are committed to 'cultural' nationalism while our 'civic' nationalism is committed to a Group of Eight state, it is possible, though not necessary, that we work against redistributive social justice in the 'culturally' chosen nation. Possible, even probable, but not necessary. Nationalism will give us no evaluative category here, if nationalism is confused with location. In other words, and I am giving you an Indian example, the NRI— Indian shorthand for the non-resident Indian— or the PIO—person of Indian origin, given certain visa privileges by India (both describing the metropolitan diasporic only in the United States and perhaps in Britain)—is not necessarily good or bad. The issue is confused by the fact that the nationalist left, the social-movement nationalist, who is now of course committed into national civil society, and the globalist-nationalist will compute 'good' and 'bad' differently. This is also going to happen, this is round the corner, vis-à-vis the Bulgarian nation-state, if and when you enter the EU. This is an interested remark of course, for I am almost an NRI. But not only an interested remark. It is also to indicate the power and danger of taking 'nationalism' as an unambiguous value today, or indeed ever. Today, when one section in the nation-state works hand in glove with the self-selected moral entrepreneurs of 'international civil society', how will the touchstone of nationalism alone allow us to read the situation, let alone act on it? An analysis of the lasting social productivity of disease- and poverty-eradication movements would be beyond the scope of this essay. Here I will simply repeat that nationalism is a deceptive category. In the early nineteenth century, when Britain was entering capitalism, Shelley wrote: 'We want the creative faculty to imagine that which we know.'[1] I will turn that much quoted lamentation on its head: 'We lack the cognitive faculty to know nationalism, because we allow it to play only with our imagination, as if it is knowledge.' At this point, as I will keep on insisting, we must train the imagination to be tough enough to test its limits. In globalized postcoloniality, we can museumize national-liberation nationalism—good for exhibitions, great exhibitions; we can curricularize national-liberation nationalism—good for the discipline of history. Learn about Nehru and Gandhi. The task for the imagination is not to let the museum and the curriculum provide alibis for the new civilizing missions, make us mischoose our allies. This whole business of redefining Eurasia. . . . One of you asked if we were jealous—Eurasia is becoming the place where NATO plays. It is not a question of jealousy but a question of fear, of Radio Free Europe saying, 'Yes, of course, the United States is a Central Asian power.' There is Turkey, entering Europe, but you are European in a different way for the rest of the world. Although you are not sufficiently European by your own count, because what you call Europe provincializes you. It's like Australia—they feel that they are provincialized by Europe. But if you look at the Australian Aboriginals, they don't think so. In Asia, the question is how we choose allies.

I want to end by speaking of the reinvention of the state. The phrase 'nation-state' rolls off our tongue. It is the reinvention of the civic state in the so-called Global South, free of the baggage of nationalist identitarianism, and inclining towards a critical regionalism, beyond the national boundaries, that seems today to be on our agenda. *You* are extraordinary in terms of regionalist possibilities, inherent in the history of your changing frontiers. To *our* inability to write anything but national allegories, and our fate to be merely parochial, has been added a new problem: 'the presuppositions of post-structuralism and its paradoxical latently identitarian anti-identitarianism, its minoritarian anti-statism, and its lack of a utopian anticapitalist critical horizon . . .'. How can these words be applied to a philosopher who has read Marx as a messianist, who has written endlessly of a democracy to come?

As for me, I am altogether utopian. I look towards a re-imagined world that is a cluster in the Global South, a cluster of regions. Of course it can only happen gradually. But as we make small structural adjustments, we should keep this goal in mind. It may produce imaginative folk who are not only going on about cultural identity (read 'nationalism'), but turning around the adverse effects of the adjustment of economic structures. The state, as Arendt says, is an abstract structure. And you may have noticed that everything I say turns around learning and teaching. One of the many tasks of the teacher of the humanities is to keep the abstract and reasonable civic structures of the state free of the burden of cultural nationalism. To repeat: an imagination trained in the play of language(s) may undo the truth-claims of national identity, thus unmooring the cultural nationalism that disguises the workings of the state—disguises the loss of civil liberties, for example, in the name of the American 'nation' threatened by terror. Again, 'may'. I will never be foolish enough to claim that a humanities education alone (especially given the state of humanities education today) can save the world! Or that anything can, once and for all. Or, even, that such a phrase or idea as 'save the world' can be meaningful.

My main topic has been the de-transcendentalizing of nationalism, the task of training the singular imagination, always in the interest of taking the 'nation' out of nation-state, if I may put it that way. Such a plan sounds bad right after national liberation. When I spoke in South Africa in the first memorial lecture after the lifting of Apartheid at a distinguished university—and I spoke of such plans—my message was not exactly popular. Then, about 10 years later, my lecture was included in an anthology and the editor wrote, 'Gayatri Spivak was prescient to have spoken at that time of the abuse of the enlightenment from below.' At the time, though, it didn't sound nice; it was too negative. This is why I am saying again and again—translate from someone who has had 60 years of independence. Translate, see if it will translate or not, rather than simply saying, 'We cannot afford to think of the nation in that way now.' That's not the point, and this is where the comparative business comes in. Hence a few obvious words about reinventing the state, words that take us outside of an education only in the humanities, are not out of place here.

Economic restructuring, as we know, removes barriers between national and international capital so that the same system of exchange can be established globally. Put so simply, there need not be anything wrong with it. Indeed, this was the fond hope of that long lost mirage, international socialism.

But the individual states are themselves in such a predicament that their situation should be transparent. Mere nationalism, ignoring that economic growth is not automatic redistributive justice, can lead us astray here. Theatrical or philanthropic wholesale counter-globalism, whatever that might be—Seattle, Genoa—is not a guarantee of redistributive justice either. It has long been my view, especially as a feminist, that even liberationist nationalisms should treat a seamless identity as something thrust upon them by the opposition. In this context, Edward

W. Said's rejection of the two-state solution in Palestine is exemplary.

Even before the advent of economic re-structuring, anyone working in the areas I spoke of could have told you that constitutional sanctions do not mean much here. But now, with state priorities increasingly altered, redistributive justice through constitutionality is less and less easy if not impossible. Philanthropy is now coming top-down from the international civil society; the state is being *de facto* (and sometimes *de jure*) un-constitutional, because it is asked to be managerial and take free-market imperatives; Human Rights Watch notices it and then the philanthropic institutions intervene. We in the South cannot usually engage constitutionally to achieve much—how can Habermas speak about constitutional patriotism, sitting in Germany, in a post-national world? It is unmindful of the current status of the world.[2] As for patriotism, even more than nationalism, it is an affect that the abstract structure of a functioning state harnesses largely for defense: *Dulce et decorum est pro patria mori*. I am back humming that childhood song from *Mebar Patan*, composed in gallant yet ideologically tarnished national liberationism: take up arms!

It is this effortful task, of keeping the civic structure of the state clear of nationalism and patriotism, altering the redistributive priorities of the state, creating regional alliances, rather than going the extra-state or non-government route alone, that the new Comparative Literature, with its alliances with the social sciences, can work at ceaselessly. This includes the reading of the past as well. I think feminist teachers of the humanities have a special role here. For behind this rearrangement of desires —the desire to win in the name of a nation—is the work of de-transcendentalizing the ruse of analogizing from the most private sense of unquestioning comfort to the most ferocious loyalty to named land, a ruse that uses and utilizes the axioms of reproductive heteronormativity. Emmanuel Levinas, for example, offers us the ruse as the establishment of a norm —the feminine establishing home as home— leading to the masculine exchange of language —which inexorably led, for Levinas, to a politics of a most aggressive nation-statism, anchored in a myth of identitarianism long predating the historical narrative of the rise of nations.[3]

In August 2003, at the public hearing of crimes against women in Bangladesh, the jury had suggested (I was part of the jury) that the

SAARC, or the South Asian Association for Regional Cooperation, be requested to put in place trans-state jurisdiction so that perpetrators can be apprehended with greater ease, and survivor-friendly laws can support trafficked women, often living with HIV/AIDS, across state lines. Such feminist work would not only supplement the rich cultural mulch of the testifying women themselves, re-coding their lives through sex-work collectives working to monitor and advise, it would also, by supporting the sex-work awareness of these women, provide an active criticism of the reproductive heteronormativity that is making the United States withdraw aid from the most successful HIV-AIDS programmes—as in Brazil or Guatemala—because they will not criminalize prostitution.[4] There, the multilingual and regional comparative work would be immensely productive.

In conclusion—a bare-bone summary. Nationalism negotiates with the most private in the interest of controlling the public sphere. I learn the lesson of equivalence rather than nationalist identitarianism from the oral-formulaic. I owe a conversation with Etienne Balibar when he suggests that equivalence masks difference whereas equality acknowledges it. I cannot quite agree with him, though I do see his point. This leads me to propose a multilingual Comparative Literature of the former empires which will arrest the tide of the creolization of native literatures.[5] This will not compromise the strength of writing in English. Higher education in the humanities should be strengthened so that the literary imagination can continue to de-transcendentalize the nation and shore up the redistributive powers of the regionalist state in the face of global priorities. Imagine this,

please, for a new world around the corner.
Thank you.

ALEXANDER KIOSSEV. Dear guests and colleagues, it was a brilliant lecture, full of unexpected jumps and heuristic shifts, I am sure that there are a lot of questions. On the other hand, to discuss this brilliant talk right away is not easy. I don't know whether somebody is ready to address the whole structure of the arguments. Nevertheless, I am sure that, at the beginning, there are at least, let's say, partial questions. Let us start with them and, in the meantime, maybe someone will be brave enough to ask about the whole structure of the argument. The floor is open.

FROM THE AUDIENCE. My question concerns the imagination, the literary imagination. If I understood correctly, when you talked about the appropriation of the mother tongue, of the first language, you described it in terms of not just appropriation, but something like ex-appropriation, which forbids such a distance from your own . . . Am I right?

GAYATRI CHAKRAVORTY SPIVAK. Something like that, yes.

FROM THE AUDIENCE. This is what permits the play of the imagination, if I can say so. What if there is no conscious distance between you and your own first language, which will not permit you an imaginative act? For example, what if the literary imagination is not the imagination of the people?

GAYATRI CHAKRAVORTY SPIVAK. Yes, it is a wonderful question, excellent question. I was really talking only to my own group—in other words, teachers of humanities. I have learned something from people who in fact have a less intimate relationship with the official language, perhaps. I am not learning nationalism from them. Given their situation, they are bilingual in what they think is their own language, which is a Creole and a version of Bengali. They switch constantly and some try to teach Bengali. But the imagination I was talking about related to people of my own kind all over the world, people who teach Comparative Literature, people who teach the Humanities, people who are in the Commonwealth Association, people who think about the fact that an empire of some kind has come to an end. I learned something about Comparative Literature practice by reading what they were doing. But the imagination can operate in other ways as well, and not just through the training of the literary imagination which is what we do. It is possible that in social formations that are defective for capitalism, for example, in Muslim communities that are not mobilized for violent action against state terrorism right now, the old responsibility-based structure called *al-haq*, a difficult word to translate, might give an imaginative purchase rather than literary language. That powerfully ambiguous word is often translated as 'truth' but it is also 'right', 'birthright'. It is the birthright of being able to take care of other people. On the other hand, what happens in these situations, and not just with Muslim communities, is that such access to the imagination becomes inoperative because the cultural semiotics are withdrawn from the mainstream, from the social productivity of capital. In that theatre, the effort is to build infrastructure, to build a different kind of education, small work, but important work. Otherwise, because reproductive heteronormativity is the oldest and broadest institution in the world, responsibility-based structures become gender-compromised. This is not the place where I go to teach literary imagination, no, I am talking about tertiary education at universities, teaching Comparative Literature. In fact, I want to connect the language-learning initiative that I am trying to put in place, since I direct an Institute for Comparative Literature and Society, with these other kinds of work. There, what you have to do is to learn from

below what philosophy of education will sur-
vive in order to give an intuition of the public
sphere without being destroyed by the others
around them who do not want them to rise.
That's a very different kind of teaching.

ALEXANDER KIOSSEV. I would like to risk
addressing just one point of your presentation:
when you spoke about your personal utopia to
detach the state, the civic state, from cultural
nationalism and to form certain regional hetero-
genic structures. I thought to myself that maybe
Bulgaria and post-socialist Bulgaria is a realiza-
tion of your utopia, because in fact the Bulgarian
state practically abdicated from any national cultural policy. And the most important Bulgarian
state institutions are imitating nationalism, they
are not really nationalistic. They are repeating
nationalistic rituals, but these rituals are empty
of any content. What happened is not a kind of

civic paradise, but that nationalism was appropriated by understate structures, corporations, soccer fans, historians, a lot of different groups with different images. And what happens is that on this, let's say, under-public level, we have a lot of nationalisms in the plural. These nationalisms are feelings, strange mass feelings, which could be called populism. Recently, a party emerged which addressed these populist nationalistic feelings. All of a sudden, this party became very powerful. I believe this is not only a Bulgarian case. I can give you German examples, I can give you Austrian examples, and Hayder and his party and a lot of other examples —Belgium, France . . . So in case the state abdicates from this traditional nationalistic politics, these feelings, call them nationalistic, call them patriotic, they just don't disappear. And it is very interesting what happens with them when certain groups and certain leaders appropriate these feelings with different causes.

GAYATRI CHAKRAVORTY SPIVAK. Yes, this is a very good warning. We think this way, to counter the international civil society, which has no democratic social contract at all. It calls itself 'civil society' simply because it is not the state, before it used to call itself 'non-governmental', but that is negative, so it gradually became 'civil society'. But what you are saying is absolutely correct. We want the state to be mindful of its redistributive obligations. As for nationalisms coming up everywhere, we are thinking about that old formula, a persistent critique. There are already existing regionalist organizations. The World Bank and the International Monetary Fund, when they began, wanted to create something like a welfare world outside of the socialist camp. Very quickly their imperatives changed.

When they began, they too were regionalists because of this kind of imperative—the importance of regions rather than state boundaries. The World Bank's Indus Valley water imperative, for example, did not honour India and Pakistan, it was the whole Indus Valley. Today, there is no way that it would not honour a national boundary. There was a flood action programme in Bangladesh, although India holds the sources of those rivers. It is no surprise that, in Asia, regionalist organizations are largely economic. What we are trying to do is to re-code these regions outside of—again that's why I like Arendt—the state boundaries, undermining the call for nationalism as ancient birth because the regions are diversified. This call will come all the time, and that's why I am trying to say how important this affect is. It is not even an affect, it's the most underived private. And it's not going to go away, hence the word 'utopia'. It's not as if you will bring the kingdom of heaven into the world by just keeping the state abstract. But what we are talking about is that there should be an effort. For that there has to be nationalist stuff elsewhere—in curricula, in museums. I agree with you, it's too dangerous, it will come back. But clean nationalism outside of an identification with the state is also part of something that we do through languages, de-transcendentalizing the nation, etc. I don't think utopia will come, because it doesn't come, it is always 'to come', as it were. It is a dangerous project, only less dangerous than the nationalist state in hock to globalization, making it rise against redistribution.

FROM THE AUDIENCE. So would you say that de-transcendentalizing the nation, we will re-transcendentalize the future? Because my intuition will be that once you step back from this transcendental meaning of the nation, you give it back to some other type of rituals. The nation-state collapses and then something comes back. Do you imagine a world without transcendental idols?

ALEXANDER KIOSSEV. To redistribute the transcendental.

GAYATRI CHAKRAVORTY SPIVAK. This is why I do believe that something like a literary training, which used to be given through cultural instruction, is a very important thing today. When I say the literary imagination de-transcendentalizes, when you think of something as literature, you don't believe in it and yet you're moved. Martin Luther King gave a great speech in 1967 at Riverside Church in New York: 'Beyond Vietnam'. In that speech he says: 'Have they forgotten that my ministry is in obedience to the One who loved his enemies so fully that he died for them?'6 For him, it was a transcendental narrative. For me, it's a narrative. But narrative is an important thing to a literary person—that's de-transcendentalizing. So that's why I'm saying that work must go on, that's why I am saying the work of the humanities is not just a little cherry on a cake, while people do speed work and the world financializes the globe. There is that, too. The de-transcendentalization is therefore a kind of training that should become part of this radical movement.

FROM THE AUDIENCE. But there is no positive element to your programme.

GAYATRI CHAKRAVORTY SPIVAK. I say *de*-transcendentalization, ok, I could find a positive word. But there is a positive element in so far as this impulse, which I also call comparativist equivalence (my mother when she said, 'It is also a mother tongue'), brings people together, that's not a negative thing. In fact, one of the things that feminists from India and Pakistan do is undo Partition. A bringing-together kind of enterprise. In these areas of the world, regional enmity is quite long-standing; therefore, that would be the positive thing. And when I'm describing what the imagination does, I have for a moment this negative word—de-transcendentalizing. I teach in New York in the most powerful university in what some call the most powerful city in the world. And I don't teach South Asia—I teach English, the language of the dominant. The students, undergraduates in my class, go on to Silicon Valley or become powerful in politics or, these days, want to help the world—human rights. It is them that I am also thinking about, not just people who are going to want something positive. These people are so ready, these children of the superpower, thinking that they are the best—it doesn't matter what colour they are—they are the reason why history happened and they can help the whole world. Take my words contextually, please—I teach in the United States among the elite and I teach in India among the subalterns. I can't speak to the whole world wanting a positive programme, but what I am asking for in this de-transcendentalization thing is a deeply positive thing—to rid the mind of the narrowness of believing in one thing and not in other things. That's what I am talking about. And the future is indeed somewhat transcendentalized in this account, if we take it on the model of Kant's transcendental deduction, as a move needed to think something unavailable to evidence but necessary for experience to be possible.

ZORNITSA HRISTOVA. I would like to ask you to say a little bit more about these multilingual comparative studies. What is the added benefit of such multilingual comparative studies with regard to the existing representation of foreign languages in the university curriculum? It is already on the programme, the vernacular languages are being studied and their literatures are studied as well. What is the added benefit of including the comparative as well?

GAYATRI CHAKRAVORTY SPIVAK. To do it comparatively is to get a sense of the global! When the powerful languages are taken as the language of translation and people read only in those powerful language translations, the fact of being translated disappears. This is not a helpful thing—because when we teach at universities, we want to be correct and this is incorrect. It is bad academic work—that people should read

Plato's *Republic* and not know that Plato did not think of republics and that it was only the Romans, who thought of 'res publica', but in Plato's work it was called something else. If you read Aristotle's *Poetics* in English, you see imitation and poetry but you don't have a sense that Aristotle is actually doing a kind of rhythmic thing with these people who might write tragedies—mimesis, poesis, mimesis, poesis.

But, indeed, if you want a broader context . . . I will tell you a story. I am in China a lot these days, because I am very interested in the Asia Pacific. And as you know, I have been learning Chinese for the last four years. The only way that I can do this, since I go there as an individual, is to find people who will allow you to come in. Why should they allow you? I am not doing anything for Columbia University —I am another Asian and my passport is

Indian. It is amazing—if you are with an NGO—cool, but by yourself . . . So one of the things that I am obliged to do is give many kinds of talks at 20-minutes' notice. Most of the time I am asked to speak to people about teaching English. I have never taught English language and I teach people whose mother tongue is English mostly, but I do it. At a certain point, I am talking to managing directors, people from the provincial government, who were learning English because of the WTO. So one guy says to me: 'Oh yes, it is because you were owned by the English, that you speak English so well.' So I say to him: 'Brother, you are absolutely right. They had their boot on our neck and so we learned to speak English well. But don't let the Americans do the same to you, ok? Don't learn English just because you want to enter the WTO. And you know why I can love English?

It is because I love my mother tongue equally.'
I didn't give him comparativism at this step, but
came close, this way: 'You know why you
should learn a language? You should learn a language so that you can read the poetry in that
language. Then you'll defeat the damn Americans. *I* am learning Chinese so that I can read
your wonderful poetry.'

I don't know if anybody here has read an
anthropologist called Elton Becker, University
of Michigan. He has an idea—in a book called,
Beyond Translation—a notion of lingual memory, very important in war and peace-making.
In order to be able to enter another space, and
globalization enters other spaces constantly, you
have to learn a language well enough to enter
its lingual memory. A fantastic idea. In the *New
York Times*, there is a little series of formulas—
how you speak to an Iraqi to convince him or

her that you are a friendly person rather than an attacking soldier. I am afraid that those kinds of formulas, unless these Iraqis are presumed to be totally stupid, do not go too far. Michael Ignatieff said that on the desks of American officials in Kabul are little tags that tell you how to say 'thank you', 'not today', etc. These people do it badly, assuming that the other is a fool. On the other hand, entering the lingual memory of subordinate languages perhaps makes for the imagining of a just world. I heard Simon Weathergood, an NGO person who works in Sri Lanka, say: 'Well, you know over the last five–six years, I've been learning both Tamil and Sinhala and I now no longer feel that I have the same goals that I came in with.' 'Just don't change. Don't change, so few people do this,' I said to him in reply. If you have a good functioning foreign language situation at your university, where the vernaculars are taught well, you should be very grateful and your university is fortunate and you are fortunate. To introduce a comparativist viewpoint will enhance the democratic spirit.

FROM THE AUDIENCE. I was thinking, while I was listening to your wonderful presentation and while I was trying to grasp the ideas during the first half an hour, about another brilliant Indian writer Arundhati Roy and her very deep novel *The God of Small Things*. Actually this is a novel about everything important in life—about death, about love and about nation as well and national culture. It is a novel in defence of local languages, local cultures, but of course written in English and due to this fact it became famous around the world. So how would you comment on this fact that actually this is pro-nationalistic, but at the same time written in a global language.

GAYATRI CHAKRAVORTY SPIVAK. Assia Djebar, whom I admire greatly, writes in French, although she is Algerian. But in the first page of her book *Women of Algiers in their Apartments,* she writes about the obligation of the stars. She says that the starry women are always called but they should become aware of what they are doing. The distance between the stars and the people is so great that the movements work because they adore their leaders. I am more interested in what is being written and not noticed and not read in the many Indian literatures. I root for comparativism there as well.

TATYANA STOYCHEVA. When we were talking about the nation-state project and the fact that it should be restructured, you also referred to Comparative Literature and the fact that it will become multilingual and apparently address new areas. But thinking about Comparative

Literature emerging in the context where national literatures emerged and there being such tight connection between the two—wouldn't you expect Comparative Literature to restructure as well in the future? What would you anticipate or suggest?

GAYATRI CHAKRAVORTY SPIVAK. Probably. I am not imaginative enough to predict. Comparative Literature, as established by the folks who came to the US after the Second World War, was already regionalist in impulse. But whereas for René Wellek it was only that which pertained to the rhetorical text itself which was up for study, now it involves the social text as well. Perhaps that's the way it will go, Tanya. But, sure, Comparative Literature will change. We are not thinking of restructuring the state, but reinventing the state as what it always is supposed to be—the mechanics of redistribution.

Restructuring is happening with neoliberalism, so that the imperatives become, supposedly free market, which is as free as all the regulations imposed by the great companies themselves, and the protectionisms written into World Trade. In the global North, it is the dismantling of the welfare state. And, of course, we haven't touched upon globalization and the digital. How a literary discipline changes in step with such conjunctural changes will become abreactively evident.

TATYANA STOYCHEVA. A rebirth of a discipline after the crisis?

GAYATRI CHAKRAVORTY SPIVAK. *Death of a Discipline* was written only about the United States. I tend always to speak in context, I always carry the trace of what I do, where I am. My books are not universal messages. A French reviewer wrote, 'Gayatri Spivak should have written this book in Bengali.' I write a lot in Bengali, but he can't read it! The situation of Comparative Literature is not the same in West Bengal! Every declaration of death, every elegy, says at the end that the person is reborn. *Death of a Discipline* is an elegy to Comparative Literature rather than simply an obituary.

So is that it? Thank you for your wonderful questions, wonderful questions!

ALEXANDER KIOSSEV. Everybody is exhausted. Before expressing my deep thanks to Prof. Spivak, I will risk something quite personal. She started with an appeal that we should translate for ourselves her presentation and I did so for myself. It was a less than sophisticated translation, because I was unable to follow everything. Some stuff I really understood, other things I am still thinking about, some others remain a little vague for me, but I have experimented with a kind of comic summary of your lecture. So I would summarize the lecture in this way and this is my personal risk—it has nothing to do with the lecture itself: 'Dear nations'—this is the general message—'dear nations, please, you were invented as imaginary narratives. After that, unfortunately you were institution-alized and you forgot your origin, you forgot that you are imaginary. Be kind enough, go back to the imaginary. You are fictive narratives and further more, please, be kind enough to compare yourselves. Then you will understand that you are not equal, you are equivalent.'

GAYATRI CHAKRAVORTY SPIVAK. Well done! Well done! You know what you forgot? Repro-ductive heteronormativity. And perhaps you mistook me for Ben[edict] Anderson? Other-wise—beautifully done! I needn't have given the lecture, it takes two minutes!

Notes

1 Percy Bysshe Shelley, 'A Defence of Poetry' (1821). Posthumously published in *Percy Byshhe Shelley, Essays, Letters from Abroad, Translations and Fragments* (ed. Mary Wollstonecraft Shelley) (London: Edward Moxon, 1840), pp. 1–57.

2 Jürgen Habermas, 'Citizenship and National Identity: Some Reflections on the Future of Europe', *Praxis International* 12.1 (1992): 1–19.

3 Emmanuel Levinas, *Totality and Infinity: An Essay on Exteriority* (Alphonso Lingis trans.) (Pittsburgh: Duquesne University Press, 1969), pp. 154–6.

4 The role of the Oscar-winning documentary *Born into Brothels: Calcutta's Red Light Kids* (2004; dirs Ross Kauffman and Zana Briski) in misrepresenting the situation—and a good deal of it through lack of access to verbal idiom—is something that could be discussed here.

5 I am not speaking of the wonderful idea of creolity that emerges from the work of Édouard Glissant (*Caribbean Discourse: Selected Essays*,

Michael Dash trans., Charlottesville: University of Virginia Press, 1989; *Poetics of Relation*, Betsy Wing trans., Ann Arbor: University of Michigan Press, 2003; Jean Bernabé et al. eds, *Éloge de la créolité*, M. B. Taleb-Khyar trans., Paris: Gallimard, 1993; Maryse Condé and Madeleine Cottenet-Hage eds, *Penser la créolité,* Paris: Karthala, 1995). I have asked the entire discipline of Comparative Literature to take creolity as its model in 'World Literature and the Creole'. Here I speak of creolization, in the narrow sense, from above, a compromising of our many mother tongues.

6 Martin Luther King, 'Beyond Vietnam: A Time to Break Silence'. Delivered 4 April 1967 at a meeting of Clergy and Laity Concerned at Riverside Church, New York. Available at: www.americanrhetoric.com/speeches/mlkatimetobreak-silence. htm